# Witley Court
## HEREFORD AND WORCESTER

### RICHARD GRAY,
*with contributions by Jeremy Musson and Shirley Evans*

*Witley Court is now a vast and spectacular ruin but 100 years ago it was one of the great Victorian country houses of England, set in elaborate formal gardens. Its splendid ostentation was an illustration of how the profits of great industries, such as coal-mining and iron-smelting, could be used to create vast country houses.*

*What you see today are largely the remains of the house and gardens created between 1854 and 1860 by William Humble Ward, later the first Earl of Dudley. His architect, Samuel Whitfield Daukes, remodelled an existing house in the fashionable Italianate style. The gardens were laid out by the prestigious designer William Andrews Nesfield.*

*Beneath the nineteenth-century skin lies an earlier structure. The core of the existing house probably dates from around 1600. In 1655 the estate was bought by Thomas Foley of Stourbridge, whose descendants reconstructed and extended much of the house during the early eighteenth century, also building the adjacent baroque parish church. A hundred years later they commissioned the architect John Nash to erect the great porticos on either side of the house. In 1837 Witley was purchased for the future Earl of Dudley, and it was he who transformed Witley into the Italianate palace.*

*The second earl sold Witley Court to Sir Herbert Smith in 1920. In 1937 a fire destroyed a substantial part of the house, and both building and contents were again sold. The part-derelict house was effectively abandoned to the elements until in 1951 a government preservation order was placed on it. Witley became the responsibility of the Department of the Environment in 1972 and is now in the care of English Heritage.*

ENGLISH HERITAGE · LONDON

# Contents

*A brief tour of Witley Court is given on
pages 24–25 (centre pages)*

*Published by English Heritage,
23 Savile Row, London W1S 2ET
Copyright © English Heritage 1997
First published by English Heritage 1997,
reprinted 1999, 2000*

*Photographs by English Heritage Photographic Unit
and copyright of English Heritage unless otherwise stated*

*Printed in England by The Colour House*
KJ   C80   11/00   FA6044
*ISBN 1 85074 472 6*

# The Challenge of Looking at Witley Court

*Witley Court in its ruined state presents an unparalleled opportunity to explore the structure of a great country house*

Although Witley Court is preserved today in a ruined state, its huge form nevertheless strikes the eye as a structure of emphatic scale and grandeur. The remaining walls and ornament of this once great country house are, in their way, still a monument to the wealthy families who owned it, extending and enhancing it from the early seventeenth century to the 1860s. But the ruins tell the story of more than just one house and one family: they are also symbolic of the fortunes of England's great country houses, many of which have been lost to unsympathetic conversions, neglect or demolition. A tall, roofless building such as Witley Court may at first seem a melancholy sight to all but the most hardened visitor, but the ruins are at the same time an astonishing opportunity to exercise the imagination, to fill the still enclosed spaces with scenes part imagined, and part informed. Witley is an open theatre for reflection, the passing of each day, and the changing seasons over the gardens and landscape, providing the natural scene changes.

Why is Witley Court as it is? The simple answer is a fire. On the evening of 7 September 1937, while the house's then owner, Sir Herbert Smith, a Kidder-

*Witley smouldering after fire*

minster carpet manufacturer, was away, flames broke out in the vicinity of the butler's pantry. Only a handful of staff were in the house, and although much of the contents was saved, the central and eastern portion of the building was substantially burnt out. A fortuitous change of wind is said to have saved the adjoining parish church, which survives in use today. The west wing, stable block and conservatory also survived the fire. After this disaster Sir Herbert put the house and estate up for auction, along with much of the contents. In the following years the surviving parts of the house, which stood empty during the years of the Second World War, were continuously stripped of saleable fittings, ironwork and slates. It was not until 1972 that Witley Court was taken into the care of the Department of the Environment.

Fires have often been significant moments in the history of great houses. Sometimes they have led to major rebuilding in a new taste. After the first quarter of the twentieth century, however, the future of country houses, erected and added to with such seeming confidence in the preceding centuries, became much more doubtful, and a major fire was likely to lead all too quickly to immediate demolition. The resulting losses included buildings which in themselves represented great landmarks in the development of English architecture, such as Roger Pratt's Coleshill in Berkshire, burned out and demolished in 1952. Powerscourt in Ireland caught fire in 1974, ironically during the Victoria and Albert Museum's exhibition entitled *The Country House: Can it Survive?*, giving vivid focus to the destruction or abandonment of many historic houses and the dispersal of their contents. Powerscourt stood empty and roofless for over twenty years, a shell but still the architectural centrepiece to terraced gardens of spectacular quality. It has recently been re-roofed but awaits full restoration.

*Coleshill, Berkshire – an important early work of Sir Roger Pratt demolished in 1958 after a fire*

*Uppark, Sussex, ravaged by fire in 1989*

*Uppark restored and reopened in 1996*

Between the 1970s and the 1990s there has been a sea-change in the nation's attitude to historic buildings generally, and to country houses in particular. A wide cross-section of the population has recognised that, as William Morris said of ancient buildings, 'These things once lost can never be replaced'. In recent years, great fires have led to great restorations. Uppark, rebuilt by the National Trust, and the restoration of Hampton Court by the Historic Royal Palaces Agency, have marked high points in terms of the value placed on these buildings for future generations, the skills available to preserve them, and, ironically, our understanding of the history of the buildings themselves. Witley Court, preserved as a ruin, illustrates something therefore of the low ebb at which such expensive and ambitious buildings found themselves in the middle of the twentieth century. The ruined house also gives some mark against which to judge the advances of our own time in the appreciation and understanding of historic buildings. Nor should any visitor fail to notice the exciting challenges that it presents English Heritage, in terms of conservation and preservation.

The opportunity to explore a ruined nineteenth-century house on the scale of Witley Court is unparalleled in this country. It allows us to look inside the structure to see elements of the Jacobean house, as well to experience vividly the sequence of architectural spaces formed by the individual rooms. The appreciation of ruins has been an important part of western culture for centuries. In one

*The exploration of ruins has long been an important part of European visual culture*

famous sixteenth-century Italian guidebook the author observed of the great classical ruins of ancient Rome: '*Roma quanta fuit ipsa ruina docet*' ('From the ruins we learn the greatness that was Rome'). The exaggerated respect for such ruins has been one of the great aesthetic influences on western culture since that period. In our own country, the ruins of medieval monastic buildings, part-destroyed at the time of the Dissolution, have also been a significant influence on British taste since the eighteenth century. The views of different generations are reflected in a different value placed on the past at any one time.

Inevitably, the way that today's visitor looks at Witley will differ from the way in which that visitor's child may look at the same ruinous building in fifty years' time. What should remain unchanged is the opportunity offered by Witley Court to look at the shape and structure of what was considered one of the grandest houses of the nineteenth century, built up layer by layer around a house of about 1600, and funded principally by the profits of industry rather than landowning or agriculture. To its successive owners the house represented an investment in the social stability of an estate, as well as an opportunity to express their wealth and status through an architecture that combined a fashionable, contemporary style with the advantages of display afforded by the great country house tradition.

Witley Court in its awesome ruined state continues to be the focus for dreams and ambitions, for the private individuals who fought to save the ruins, and for those who now work on their preservation and presentation. More importantly, it continues to be visited by thousands of people every year, as it should be.

# The Owners of Witley Court

## Early history

After the Norman Conquest the land on which Witley stands was granted to Urso d'Abetot, whose ownership is mentioned in the Domesday survey of 1086. By 1100 the manor of Witley had been acquired by William de Beauchamp, becoming the property of Hugh Cooksey by the mid-thirteenth century. The medieval room in the basement of the house is thought to date from this period. Four generations of ownership by the Cookseys ended when Thomas Cooksey died in 1498; his co-heirs were the cousins Robert Winter and Robert Russell of Strensham, near Tewkesbury, and Witley was assigned to the latter. At that time the manor of Witley comprised 300 or 400 acres (120–160 hectares), a church, and the manor house (the Court).

A substantial house was built soon after Robert Russell acquired the manor, and then enlarged approximately 100 years later; formal gardens were laid out at the same time. The park is known to have been in existence by the sixteenth century. During the Civil War, Witley Court was the residence of Sir William Russell, a Royalist supporter and a High Sheriff and Governor of Worcester. In 1652 Sir William is recorded as being threatened with the forfeiture of Witley to an Edward Harrison, to whom he was in debt. The debt must have been settled promptly, for two years later Sir William gave the property to his son Thomas as a wedding present. In 1655, however, Thomas Russell sold the estate to Thomas Foley of Stourbridge. This transaction included the Court, described as 'an imposing residence' of red brick with detailing in the local red sandstone.

## The Foleys

The Foley fortune originated with Richard Foley, born in Dudley in 1580, at a time when the iron industry in the area was expanding. At first Richard sold iron nails but he later became involved in their manufacture as a forge master. Foreign competition was stiff, and Richard determined to improve the method – at that time predominantly hand-work – by which the nails were made. For this purpose he is said to have travelled to Upsala in Sweden to observe a nail-making machine. Back in England he set up a similar process but had to return to Sweden to plagiarise their system further, gaining entry to the works by pretending to be half-witted. Having thus cunningly absorbed the nail-making technology, Richard Foley established forges in the Stourbridge district. He went on to become a respected member of Dudley society, being elected mayor at the age of thirty-six and building an almshouse for the poor. He married twice, producing thirteen children, and moved to Stourbridge around 1630.

Thomas Foley, born in 1616 or 1617, was Richard's first son by his second wife Alice. Thomas further developed his father's business, doing well out of the Civil War by supplying iron cannons and their ballistics. Appropriately, he married Anne Browne of Spelmonden in Kent, daughter of the greatest gun manufacturer in the country, succeeding to a half-share in this enterprise when its founder died in 1652. Thomas Foley is reputed to have had an annual income of some £5000, a huge sum at the time, and was therefore well able to purchase the Witley estate in 1655. He was highly regarded, gaining a

*Thomas Foley, who purchased the estate in 1655*

*Anne Browne of Spelmonden, Kent, wife of the first Thomas Foley*

reputation for 'just and blameless dealing, that all men that he ever had to do with ... magnified his great integrity and honesty which was questioned by none'. Thomas engaged in local philanthropy, endowing Oldswinford Hospital, Stourbridge, a school which is still flourishing today. He became the High Sheriff of Worcestershire in 1655 and served as a member of parliament. He died in 1677.

Witley Court passed to Thomas Foley's son, also named Thomas, who similarly served as county sheriff and MP, and was the first of seven Thomas Foleys to succeed to the estate. His son Thomas Foley III, again a parliamentarian and sheriff, was created Baron Foley of Kidderminster by Queen Anne in 1711. Baron Foley carried out extensive improvements to the mansion and park, and intended to rebuild the medieval church, but he died in 1732 before work started, and the new church had to be paid for by his wife Mary, and son

Thomas, the second Baron Foley. The second baron died a bachelor in 1766 and Witley passed to Thomas V, of Stoke Edith near Hereford, a distant cousin. Thomas V continued the family tradition of parliamentary service, being elevated to the peerage as Baron Foley 'of the second creation' in 1776. His successor to the title was the colourful Thomas VI, known as 'Lord Balloon' after an incident in which a hot air balloon got out of control in the gardens of his London house. He achieved high office as a Privy Councillor and Lord Lieutenant of the county, but because of his extravagance and gambling mania he had been disinherited by his father, and the family fortune became badly eroded. The son of 'Lord Balloon', Thomas VII, inherited in 1793 when only thirteen years old. In 1806 he restored his financial position by marrying a daughter of the Duke of Leinster; the two great porticos on the north and south fronts of the Court were added around this time. By 1833,

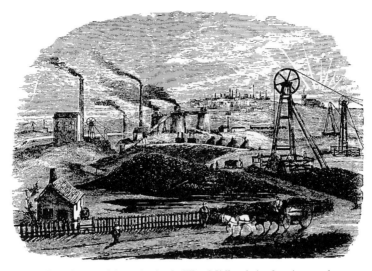

*The Dudley mines and factories in the West Midlands in the nineteenth century*

however, when Thomas VII died, the Foley reserves were again so depleted that his son had to part with Witley four years later in order to clear the debt.

*Thomas, second Baron Foley of the second creation, known as 'Lord Balloon'*

# William Humble Ward, first Earl of Dudley (1818–85)

In 1837 the trustees of William Humble Ward, eleventh Baron Ward of Birmingham and at that time a minor, purchased Witley Court for the gigantic sum of £890,000 (the equivalent today of over £32 million). Ward was one of the richest men in Britain, which at the time meant one of the wealthiest men in the world. As with the Foleys, money had been generated by enterprises in the West Midlands, but compared to the Foleys' source of wealth Lord Ward's empire, derived from the technical innovations of the Industrial Revolution, was a much greater prize. He was heir to the income from over 200 mines in the 'Black Country', from which were extracted coal, iron, limestone and fireclay. He also owned iron-smelting works, chemical factories and a railway construction business – all of which produced an annual income of some £100,000. Ward had inherited these vast assets in 1833 from a distant relation, John William Ward,

*Queen Adelaide, wife of William IV, by Franz Winterhalter. The dowager queen was a tenant at Witley from 1843–46*

first Earl Dudley and a former Foreign Secretary. Known as 'the Lorenzo of the Black Country' – presumably a reference to Lorenzo de Medici – the earl died insane, conversing with himself in two voices, one falsetto, one bass.

Lord Ward did not come into his full inheritance until the age of 28, and until then lived at the family home of Himley Hall near Stourbridge. Witley Court was let, its most notable tenant, from 1843–46, being Queen Adelaide, widow of King William IV. The queen appears to have been a popular figure locally and was frequently to be seen driving out in her carriage. She had the first village school erected in Great Witley.

Witley became Lord Ward's home in 1846 and in 1851 he married a society beauty, Selina Constance de Burgh; however, she died in childbirth the same year in Germany. Soon afterwards he began planning the transformation of Witley into a seat befitting a millionaire industrialist and work started three years later, continuing until 1860 when the gardens and fountains were completed. The total cost is said to have exceeded £250,000 (almost £10 million at today's values). In the same year, the earldom of Dudley was resuscitated and conferred on Lord Ward in recognition of his beneficence to local charities. In 1865 he married Georgina Elizabeth Moncreiffe, by whom he had six sons and one daughter.

*William Humble Ward, first Earl of Dudley, the creator of Victorian Witley*

*Georgina Elizabeth Moncreiffe, first Countess of Dudley*

*Himley Hall, the Dudley home near Stourbridge*

Apart from Witley Court, the Dudley family owned or leased another fourteen properties or estates during the late nineteenth century. In addition to Himley Hall, there were Dudley Castle and Priory near Birmingham; Dudley House and 7 Carlton Gardens in London; Dunkeld House and Ednam in Scotland; Rockingham Castle in Roscommon and Screeb Lodge on Lough Corrib in County Galway, Ireland; Croggen House in north Wales; an estate at Malpas in Cheshire; two houses in France, at Boulogne and Nice; and a plantation in Jamaica. In addition the first earl owned homes in Rome and Vienna and the second earl possessed a yacht. By 1883 the Dudley estates totalled 25,554 acres (10,300 hectares), over 14,000 acres (5700 hectares) of which were in Worcestershire.

The lifestyle at Witley was indeed opulent; writing many years later a guest recalled a Christmas tree hung with jewels from which the ladies were invited to choose. The earl spoke Italian and was something of an expert on music. He died at the age of sixty-seven in 1885 and was succeeded by his son, also named William. Countess Georgina lived to a great age, dying in 1929. Even in old age she was famous locally for her 'stately bearing', good looks and charm.

## The second earl (1867–1932)

When the first earl died his heir was eighteen and, like his father, took up residence at the Court only on coming of

*Dudley House, Park Lane, one of the family's London residences*

age. Witley Court was the scene of lavish festivities on the occasion of his twenty-first birthday, and again when, in 1891, he married Rachel Anne Gurney, a banking heiress.

During the 1890s, Witley Court reached the zenith of its magnificence. The Prince of Wales (later King Edward VII) became a friend of the earl and a regular visitor, accompanied by an aristocratic entourage for the elaborate shooting parties that were held here. The park had a staff of twenty-five full-time gamekeepers who maintained a stock of partridges, pheasants and deer for these occasions. In 1895 the earl had a golf course laid out for the further entertainment of his guests. During these grand house-parties every inch of the mansion would be full, with guests staying for up to a week. Their

*An extensive account exists of the young earl's twenty-first birthday celebrations in 1888:*

*The second earl aged eighteen, when still Viscount Ednam*

## 7 August

At noon, the earl and his mother received an address of congratulations from tenants of the Witley Court estate. At 3 p.m. the tenants of the Holt estate tendered their felicitations.

A ball in the evening for the county was attended by 214 guests, with a 60ft (18m) marquee erected in the grounds. Both drives were illuminated by hurricane lamps, and 'fairy' lights bordered the lawns. Another marquee accommodated the guests' coachmen, while a huge temporary stable was provided for 100 horses.

## 8 and 9 August

The next day deputations of tradesmen, both local and from London, presented further congratulations in the Picture Gallery. Festivities continued for a third day. The drives were decorated with flags and bunting, and another huge marquee, over 200ft (60m) long, was erected in the park. Nearly 900 male cottagers sat down to an ample lunch washed down with plentiful supplies of beer. There was also a full-scale fair, complete with merry-go-rounds, swing-boats, Punch-and-Judy shows and demonstrations of juggling and ventriloquism. Pleasure boats floated on the lake in front of the house and the fountains played for an hour during the afternoon. A tea was served to 416 children and 427 mothers and other village women, followed by dancing to two bands. As darkness fell, the fountains were illuminated and the evening came to a climax with an elaborate firework display.

*A royal shooting party at Witley. To the left of centre stands the young countess Rachel, left of her is the earl, while the portly figure in the middle is the Prince of Wales (later King Edward VII)*

servants also had to be accommodated: gentlemen would bring a valet and ladies were accompanied by a personal maid, to organise their frequent changes of clothing during the day. Some guests even brought their own cook. The Prince of Wales, often travelling without his wife Princess Alexandra, had a large retinue which sometimes included his personal loaders for the shooting. A day of sporting activities created substantial appetites which were satisfied by lavish dinners, held, when there was a large assembly, in the ballroom or the Picture Gallery.

*Rachel, Countess of Dudley, dressed as Queen Esther for the Devonshire House ball held in July 1897 to celebrate Queen Victoria's Diamond Jubilee.* Vanity Fair *magazine wrote, 'Young Lady Dudley was brilliant as "Queen Esther" in white – no other character could have suited her so well, as her features are quite of Eastern type ...'* The Times *gave a long description of her costume, which included a chasuble (the long panel falling from her neck) of solid gold tissue encrusted with jewels, a head-dress of two veils and a crown, and fifteen large drop pearls on her forehead*

## Servants at Witley Court

At this time Witley Court had some fifty household servants, presided over by the butler. He was in charge of the indoor male staff and responsible for the service of meals, drinks and generally the smooth running of the establishment. The housekeeper took her orders from the countess and, through an army of housemaids, dealt with all cleaning duties. Of equal rank were the head cook and head gardener, both of whom had a large staff bringing the total complement to more than 100.

## The Dudleys in public and private

In 1895, at the age of twenty-eight, the earl became the Mayor of Dudley. This was followed by a succession of public appointments, including Lord Lieutenant of Ireland (the British monarch's representative before Partition) in 1902–5, Privy Councillor, and finally Governor General of Australia from 1908 to 1911.

The earl and his wife Rachel had seven children, born between 1892 (Lady Gladys Honor) and 1907 (the twins, Lords Edward Frederick and George Reginald). Viscount Ednam, the earl's heir, was born in 1894. The earl and countess were very different people. He was gregarious with an Edwardian taste for racy society, whereas Rachel set store by the solid Victorian virtues of duty, home, family and church. In 1891, before her marriage, she had organised a field hospital in South Africa for which she was awarded the CBE. She put her nursing experience to further use in France during the First World War, and throughout her life concerned herself with the sick. Eventually cracks began to appear in the marriage, and in 1908 a legal separation was drawn up, with the Court settled on the countess.

The countess took a great interest in the gardens at Witley, laying out an area with clipped topiary hedges known as 'My

PARDOE COLLECTION

*The conservatory in 1918: the twins, Lord Edward and Lord George, their sister Lady Alexandra (left) and a friend pose with the governess Miss Badham*

Lady's Garden'. A woman of diminutive stature, Rachel could nevertheless present a formidable character; on Sunday mornings, for example, she would lead her staff in a stately procession through the house to the church.

## The decline of a fortune

As a result of foreign competition the Dudley wealth was on the wane. Between 1889 and 1913, the earl is known to have mortgaged the estate and sold pictures to fund his extravagant entertaining. After the house had been sold in 1920 the urns at the foot of the main stairs were found to be stuffed with unpaid bills, carelessly tossed away by the earl as he descended to breakfast each morning. In June 1920 the family was struck by tragedy when Countess Rachel drowned in a swimming accident at the Dudleys' house in County Galway, Ireland. The need for financial retrenchment caused the earl to sell the Court, parkland and home farm in the same year. He remarried in 1924 (the former 'Gaiety girl' Gertie Millar, with whom he is said to have had a liaison in

*'My Lady's Garden', an area of clipped topiary (now disappeared) laid out for Rachel, the second countess*

the First World War), moving back to Himley where he entertained the Prince of Wales (later Edward VIII) and Wallis Simpson. The earl died in 1932, to be

succeeded by his eldest son William Humble Eric. The latter's son, William Humble David, born in 1920, is the present and fourth Earl of Dudley.

## Sir Herbert Smith

The new owner of Witley Court was yet another rich industrialist aspiring to the status of landed gentry. Herbert Smith had publicly voiced his ambition of owning the Court before the sale of 1920; in the event, it changed hands in great haste – less than three weeks from the date of Countess Rachel's death.

Born in Kidderminster in 1872, Smith worked for the ailing carpet manufacturer, Humphries, rising from designer to general manager by 1906. By way of redundancies and reorganisation he restored the firm to profitability. Four years later he purchased the company, eventually setting up a conglomerate, Carpet Trades Ltd, in 1920. In the same

*Gertrude 'Gertie' Millar, a star of the Gaiety music hall in London. She married the second earl in 1924 after his first wife had drowned*

*Sir Herbert Smith (known locally as 'Piggy'), owner of Witley Court 1920–38*

year he received a baronetcy for his services as chairman of the Carpet-Rationing Committee during the First World War. He retired in 1922, a millionaire, aged forty-nine.

Sir Herbert derived his nickname 'Piggy' from his corpulent physique. He came from a musical family and was an accomplished violinist. He acquired the Court furnished, although the Earl of Dudley had sold many items. Sir Herbert installed electricity the year after he purchased the property but, despite this investment, staff levels were reduced and parts of the house abandoned. He earned local unpopularity by trying to prevent the Worcester Hunt from crossing his land and to close off the villagers' ancient rights of way.

## The fire

The fire, which began at about 8 p.m. on 7 September 1937, brought to an abrupt close Witley Court's existence as a rich man's home. Little could be done to quell the flames since the hydrant system connected to the fountain reservoir had not been maintained, and the so-called 'fire-proof' floors installed by the architect William Daukes in the mid-nineteenth century proved ineffectual. The house's insurers would have paid for only a quarter of the cost of rebuilding, and Sir Herbert therefore decided to dispose of the property. An initial attempt to auction the whole estate failed when bidding stopped at a derisory £21,000; the impending Second

PARDOE COLLECTION

*Witley Court in 1969. Trees have grown up inside the ruined walls and the south formal garden is derelict*

*The conservatory in the 1960s. The roof has been removed but the marble floor, border edge and many of the plants survive*

World War can be blamed for the poor response. The contents and many garden ornaments were auctioned over eight days in the autumn of 1938, followed by the sale of the house itself the following year to a Mr Banks for only £4000. The park and home farm were sold off separately as parcels of agricultural land.

## Ruin and resurrection

The Court changed hands again in 1954, to an antique dealer, Mr Wigington of Stratford-upon-Avon. Anything that could be sold was stripped from the building: lead, slates and timber from the roof, marble chimneypieces from the interior, statuary from the gardens and heavy plate-glass from the conservatory. Rapidly the building turned into a ruin,

with trees growing up through the floors. During the 1950s and '60s Witley Court came close to demolition. There were proposals for a motor-racing circuit, a caravan park and a housing estate on the site. The church might have been bodily removed to London, and the Perseus and Andromeda fountain nearly graced a traffic island outside Worcester Cathedral. The Department of the Environment came to the rescue in 1972 with a compulsory guardianship order; decay was arrested and repairs made to the structure. Since its creation in 1984, English Heritage has continued the programme of improvements. The church of St Michael, which had also fallen into decay, has been the subject of a preservation campaign mounted by an energetic local 'Friends' group.

# A History of the House and Estate

*The brick house built in the early seventeenth century and purchased by Thomas Foley in 1655. This late seventeenth-century painting (the original of which is now lost) is the only existing image of Jacobean house.*

## Medieval Witley

Underneath the skin of the mid-Victorian stonework lies evidence of the earlier phases of Witley's history. Below the Entrance Hall are the remains of a vaulted stone building thought to date from the thirteenth century. (This is inaccessible to the public as it is covered by the concrete raft put in at the main floor level during the 1970s.) It seems possible that this structure was the undercroft of a solar or withdrawing chamber, which would have been located at one end of a Great Hall, the centre of a medieval manor house. The undercroft could only be entered via a spiral stair leading down from the solar, thereby creating a secure location for valuables belonging to the lord of the manor – at that time a member of the Cooksey family. The original Great Witley church, of similar date, lay slightly to the west of the present eighteenth-century church.

## The seventeenth-century house

We know little of Robert Russell's house on the site, said to have been built soon after he inherited the property in 1498. A surrounding deer park is thought to have

*The medieval basement under the Entrance Hall before it was covered by a concrete floor in the 1970s*

*Wimbledon House, Surrey, a late sixteenth-century mansion demolished in 1720. The entrance front of Witley might have been similar*

been enclosed in the first half of the sixteenth century. In about 1600 the house was rebuilt by a descendant of Russell; the result is illustrated in a late seventeenth-century painting (*above left*). The south facade (the back of the house) featured a door flanked by symmetrically placed chimneystacks. From here two long wings (not visible in the painting) projected northwards: the west wing contained a Long Gallery on the first floor, while the east wing housed the service accommodation. To the rear of the central block were twin towers, each containing staircases. The windows were of mullion-and-transom design, except for those at the

*An 'Ipswich'-type window at Charlton House in south-east London. The glazing of the windows terminating the wings on the south front at Witley was similar*

ends of the short projections on the garden front, which featured windows of the so-called 'Ipswich' type. Like many contemporary houses, Witley was built of brick with stone dressings; around the time of James I's accession to the throne in 1603, the architecture of the brick-dominated Low Countries became a fashionable influence on building design in England. A cupola or lantern is also visible in the painting – again, a typical late Elizabethan and Jacobean feature.

This house was presumably the 'imposing residence' described as having been sold to Thomas Foley of Stourbridge in 1655. With it came a 530-acre (215-hectare) park, a bowling-green meadow to the north of the house comprising some 35 acres (14 hectares), 'Mill Farm House' and surrounding lands.

Thomas Foley died in 1677 and his son, Thomas II, converted the Court into what was described by William Camden in his *Britannia* (1695) as 'a fair new-built house'. It is possible that the overhanging hipped roof and 'Ipswich' windows described above actually date from this time rather than from 1600. By 1689 Thomas II had acquired the six manors that comprise Great Witley, totalling about 2600 acres (1050 hectares).

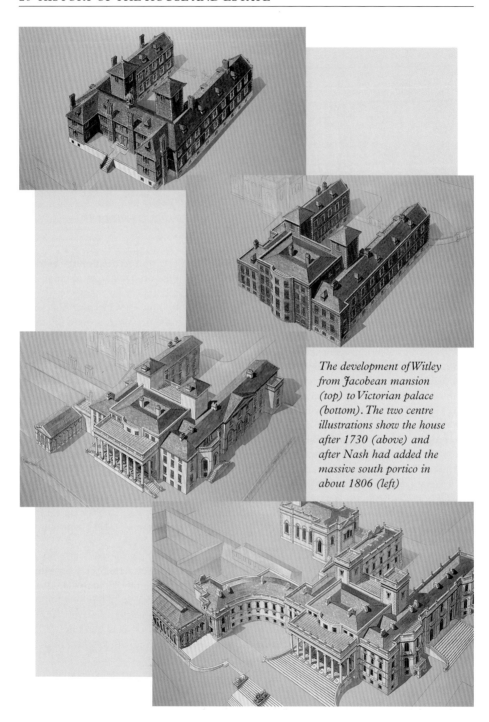

*The development of Witley from Jacobean mansion (top) to Victorian palace (bottom). The two centre illustrations show the house after 1730 (above) and after Nash had added the massive south portico in about 1806 (left)*

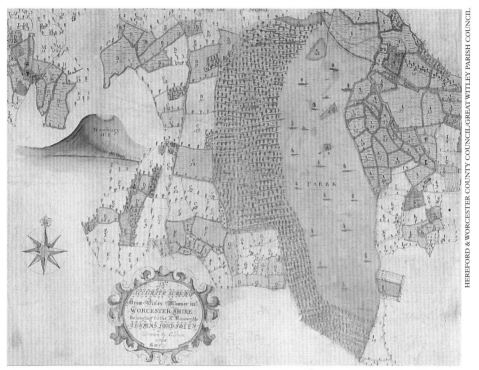

*A map of Great Witley made by Joshua Price in 1732. At the top right of the map, the old drive curves round on the north side of the house with a formal avenue of trees on the right*

## Eighteenth-century expansion

Thomas II died in 1700, to be succeeded by Thomas III, created Baron Foley of Kidderminster. In the period 1725-30 Lord Foley radically extended and modernised the house. He rebuilt the central block, raising it to create a third storey and doubling it in depth to fill in the space between the two short wings on the south front. This new garden front was also given an elegant elliptical central bow feature. New parapets extended around the roof and bay windows were added to terminate the ends of the north wings.

Lord Foley also wished to create a grand symmetrical approach to the house from the north. A map of 1732 (*above*) reveals that the entrance route more or less followed the line of the existing drive

*The mid-eighteenth-century approach to the house was by a causeway which crossed the Front Pool*

*The north front by George Repton, showing the symmetrical service wings built by Thomas, first Baron Foley in 1725–30*

from the west but then meandered around to the north side of the house; the avenue of trees shown marching away to the south-east may have been simply an ornamental feature. For this new northern drive Lord Foley purchased additional land in 1718, although the work could not have been completed until after Price made his map fourteen years later. The new drive was carried on a causeway across a lake formed from an existing ravine and stream, before arriving at the entrance front. New square service blocks, connected to the north wings by curving walls, were built to make a grand assemblage in the fashionable Palladian style. The effect was further enhanced by

*The Keeper's Lodge or Deer Park House in the late eighteenth century*

arcaded screen walls extending on either side.

Thomas III also intended to rebuild the crumbling medieval church, but his plans had to wait until after his death in 1732. The designer of the new church, consecrated in 1735, may have been the London architect James Gibbs (1682–1754) (see pages 44–6).

A remarkable feature of the Witley scene which has now totally disappeared was the Keeper's Lodge, also known as the Deer Park House. It not only acted as an 'eye-catcher' in the landscape on the south side of the house, but served as a shooting lodge and a home for the head gamekeeper and his family. The building is known to have existed in 1664. In the mid-eighteenth century it was rebuilt to the designs of a prominent London architect, Henry Flitcroft. During the nineteenth century its portico became a useful grandstand from which sporting events could be viewed. By 1938 this attractive building had become derelict and it was demolished in about 1950.

Towards the end of the eighteenth century two ice houses were constructed near the church. The ice would have been gathered in winter from the nearby newly formed lake and stored in these underground chambers until summer,

*John Nash's alternative proposal for improvements to the south front without the portico. It was eventually discarded in favour of the more ambitious design below*

when it could be used to make frozen desserts. Also about this time the walls of the mansion were given a coating of stucco.

The two great Ionic porticos on the north and south fronts of the house were added in about 1805, during the residence of Thomas VII, third Baron Foley of the second creation. For this work he employed the fashionable London architect John Nash (1752–1835). Both porticos were constructed of stone. The garden front portico, eight columns wide and two deep and raised up on a new terrace, has been described as the largest of any country house in Britain. Nash also heightened the wings so that the roof-line corresponded with the cornice on the porticos, rebuilt the roof in a flatter pitch with overhanging eaves (also applying this treatment to the towers), and demolished the service blocks on the north front, replacing them with new accommodation around two courtyards at the south-western corner of the house. The Court now reflected the prevailing taste for the 'picturesque', combining, to quote Sir John Summerson, 'the severe antique [the porticos] with casual Italian of the Cronkhill sort' [Nash's prototype villa near Shrewsbury]. This work took many years: an account written in 1814 mentions the 'unsettled state of the house'. The same writer, F C Laird, also describes Witley as 'an immense white building'. Lord Foley spent much of the already depleted family reserves on these alterations and was even forced to raise a loan from Nash on the security of Foley House in London.

*J Wood's view of 1843 showing Nash's design as executed, including the conservatory on the left (later replaced by Daukes's version)*

# A Brief Tour of Witley Court

**South parterre garden** The spectacular Perseus and Andromeda fountain formed the centrepiece of this magnificent garden *(pages 31–4)*

**Conservatory** Tropical plants flourished within the thick plate-glass walls of the conservatory or 'orangery', one of the wonders of Witley Court *(pages 43–4)*

**Louis XVI Court** Fruit trees were probably trained against the walls of this sheltered area *(page 44)*

**Stables courtyard** (not accessible to the public)

**South portico** Also by Nash, this portico offered panoramic views of the south parterre garden and the deer park beyond *(pages 42–3)*

**Drawing Room** A low-ceilinged but elaborately decorated room overlooking the gardens *(pages 41–2)*

**Dining Room** This octagonal room provided an opulent yet intimate setting for the entertainment of guests *(pages 40–1)*

**East parterre garden** This attractive garden, with its fountain and statue of the goddess Flora, formed an elegant backdrop to the Ballroom and Dining Room *(pages 34–5)*

**Church of St Michael and All Angels** The parish church of Great Witley (not in the care of English Heritage) has a remarkable baroque interior *(pages 44–6)*

**Forecourt** The grand front entrance to Witley Court, with a portico designed by John Nash in *c.*1806 *(page 37)*

**Front Pool** The relaxed tranquillity of the lake, which formed the main view from the front of the house, contrasts strikingly with the formality of Nesfield's gardens to the south and east *(pages 28–9)*

**Ballroom** The Dudleys' magnificent ballroom was flamboyantly decorated with gilded plasterwork and crystal chandeliers *(page 41)*

**Entrance Hall** Originally a Jacobean Great Hall, in the Dudley era it featured a grand staircase and brass-railed balcony *(pages 37–9)*

## Witley reaches its peak

So impoverished was the Lord Foley who succeeded to the title in 1833 that he could not enjoy Witley in its new form. Four years later he decided to accept an offer from the trustees of William Humble Ward, Baron Ward of Birmingham; however, Ward did not move to Witley until 1846. A further eight years passed before work started on transforming the Court and its grounds yet again. By the 1850s Nash's neoclassical-villa treatment of the Court had gone out of fashion. Mid-Victorian architecture polarised between the Gothic Revival and a confident classical style based on sixteenth- and seventeenth-century Italian designs. Witley in its last phase is a supreme example of the latter. The construction in 1845–48 of Osborne House on the Isle of Wight for Queen Victoria made the Italian style even more fashionable.

For this vast work of transformation Ward brought in Samuel Whitfield Daukes (1811–80). Daukes had trained with an architect in York before starting a practice in Gloucester in 1837, where he became the architect of the railway linking Gloucester with Birmingham. In about 1845–46 he rebuilt Abberley Hall near

Witley in the Italian style, and it seems likely that Ward would have been introduced to Daukes through his familiarity with the nearby house. Daukes's ambition later took him to London, where he set up practice in 1848. His only other country house is the Tudor-style Horsted Place in Sussex (1850–52).

Daukes's work at Witley Court consisted of clothing the mansion in Bath stone while leaving Nash's existing stone porticos untouched. Once again the roof was removed and replaced with a flat-pitched lead roof concealed by a balustraded parapet of the same design as those above the porticos. A new wing curved to the south-west and terminated in the so-called 'Michelangelo' Pavilion; beyond this was a huge new conservatory (sometimes known as the Orangery) which replaced a more modest version from the Nash period. The Bath stone cladding even extended to the church, which was thus brought into the overall composition. The leading garden designer of the day, William Andrews Nesfield, was employed to lay out Witley's vast formal gardens and design the centrepiece fountains (see pages 30–6).

Inside the house a fashionable cosmetic modernisation, grafted on to the existing

*Nearby Abberley Hall, by Samuel Daukes, built in 1845–46*

*The new conservatory in about 1870*

walls, was carried out by Moxons, the royal decorators. Much use was made of Carton Pierre mouldings (a kind of strengthened papier mâché – see page 29) for the walls and ceilings. The style varied between the restrained, classically inspired panelling in the Entrance Hall – designed to make a dignified impression on visitors – and the flamboyant exercise in Louis XIV baroque in the Ballroom, on the ground floor of the east wing. The fashion for opulent interiors, inspired by French decoration of the seventeenth and eighteenth centuries, appealed particularly to those made rich by the Industrial Revolution, such as Lord Ward, who, by the time he properly moved into these luxurious interiors, had been created Earl of Dudley. The Drawing Room on the south front was thoroughly French, although it suffered from poor proportions as a result of the low ceiling inherited from the original house. The Ballroom did not have this problem because the east wing had been reconstructed by Nash. Here Daukes installed a so-called fire-proof floor – which, sadly, turned out to be useless in the fire of 1937; but it did support the weight of the bedroom walls above.

The upper floor of the west wing was occupied by the Picture Gallery, a remodelling of the old Long Gallery. It had windows in the east wall and sections of the ceiling were glazed to provide additional light for the pictures.

A photographic archive and the 1938 sales catalogue provide an indication of how the interiors were furnished during the nineteenth century. The Dudleys owned some important French, Italian and Flemish items, as well as much standard mid-Victorian upholstered seating (seen in the photograph of the Picture Gallery on page 28) and reproduction pieces in the Boulle style. The first Earl of Dudley is said to have owned a substantial collection of paintings and some fine Italian Old Master drawings. Many works of art were sold by the second earl, but a substantial array survived to be recorded in a photograph of the gallery taken by the photographer Harry Bedford Lemere in 1920.

## Services and technology

'Below stairs' the basement extended under the entire house except the west wing. The large square kitchen was

*PARDOE COLLECTION*

*The Picture Gallery in the west wing in 1882*

immediately behind the grand staircase and had a glass dome in the roof. The butler's pantry lay beneath the Dining Room on the east front, while the housekeeper's room occupied the area under the Saloon and looked into the light-well under the south portico. The servants' hall stood behind the curving west wing, with the Dudley children's schoolroom above. Extending west were two service courtyards ending in the stables. Over the entrance to the stables was a small tower surmounted by a cupola containing a chiming clock; these have recently been restored. At the back of the stable yard stood a gigantic coal stack which was maintained at approximately 1500 tons (tonnes). This fed five hot-water boilers and the dozens of fireplaces in the house. A track in a tunnel connected the coal stack to a cellar below the house. One of the boilers worked a hot-air central-heating system, much in advance of its time, which warmed the house and church. On occasion the house could consume 30 tons (tonnes) of coal per day. Naturally it was Dudley coal, brought from the Black Country by barge to Shrawley and carried the remaining four miles by horse and cart. The local tenant farmers were required to perform this service in lieu of rent.

## Witley in its setting

Today it is difficult to appreciate fully the appearance of the landscape surrounding the Court, particularly on the far side of the drive, opposite the north front. This area, once quite open, provided a view of the Front Pool from the house and vice versa, but is now obscured by trees. The Pool House land was sold off after the

*NATIONAL MONUMENTS RECORD*

*A bedroom sumptuously panelled in French polished satinwood, in a photograph of 1920*

break-up of the estate, but it has recently been acquired by English Heritage. There is now no trace of the mid-eighteenth-century causeway which crossed the Front Pool, carrying the driveway to the house. This was superseded by the third Lord Foley's more conveniently aligned drives in the early nineteenth century. The interesting Red House at the western end of the Hundred Pool started life as aristocratic dog kennels, designed by George Stanley Repton in about 1828. It comprised four octagons grouped around a fifth one, with runs for the dogs. In the twentieth century it was converted to human accommodation and lost its symmetry with the addition of extensions. The lodges at the ends of the drives were not built until 1884. They were designed by Henry Rowe and Son of Worcester in French Second Empire style, each with a steeply pitched roof.

*The main entrance from the far side of the Front Pool – a view lost for half a century by uncontrolled trees but now about to be restored*

Plans for future developments at Witley focus extensively on the restoration of some elements of the nineteenth-century landscape (see pages 47–8).

## 'Carton Pierre' decoration

This was an early attempt at mass-production of decorative mouldings for walls and ceilings. It was invented in the mid-nineteenth century by Mizière, a Parisian plasterer, and was similar to papier-mâché but of a more refined composition, so that highly detailed mouldings could be created. The ingredients included shredded paper, glue, water, flour and 'whiting' – made from ground chalk. Sometimes alum (sulphate of aluminium and potassium) was added. This mixture was boiled up and then pressed into wooden or metal moulds. The resultant mouldings were then glued on to the prepared plaster surfaces.

Carton Pierre came to be used extensively and in the most fashionable circles: it featured in the Louvre and the Palais Royal in Paris. English manufacturers took up the process and it was employed in the decoration of Sandringham for the future King Edward VII. Eventually, Carton Pierre was superseded by fibrous plaster which was stronger and could be made in larger sections.

*The remains of mid-nineteenth-century 'Carton Pierre' wall decoration in the Saloon*

# The Gardens of Witley Court

*The south-east aspect of Witley Court in the early nineteenth century. Beyond Repton's terrace is an informal deer park*

In 1846 when William Humble Ward (later first Earl of Dudley) came into his inheritance, a golden age of opulence began at Witley Court which was to last until 1920 when the Court was sold by the Dudley family. Before this the land surrounding the house had been a deer park, laid out in the English landscape manner advocated by Lancelot 'Capability' Brown and his followers. When this style, with its acres of greensward, lost its appeal in the late eighteenth century, Lord Foley (Thomas VII), who owned the property from 1793–1833, asked George Stanley Repton to establish terracing and balustrading in the immediate environs of the house, with flower beds and simple parterres.

Nesfield, who was the leading landscape designer of the day, to lay out a sumptuous pleasure ground which would be a suitable accompaniment to the newly extended and refurbished Italianate mansion. Nesfield was later to describe the gardens at Witley as his 'monster work'.

## William Andrews Nesfield (1794–1881)

As part of Lord Ward's grand transformation of the mansion, it was decided to call in William Andrews

*Portrait of Nesfield by John Duffield Harding, c. 1840*

The son of a Church of England vicar, Nesfield was initially intended to follow both his father and grandfather into the Church. While at school, however, Nesfield met his cousin, an officer in the army, and decided on a change of career. After two terms at Trinity College, Cambridge, and a period at the Royal Military Academy at Woolwich, where he studied architectural perspective, engineering and mapmaking, Nesfield served first as a Second Lieutenant in the Peninsula Campaigns in Spain and then as aide-de-camp to Sir Gordon Drummond, the Commanding Officer of the Niagara Region in Canada. On his return to England Nesfield relinquished his commission to become a professional watercolour painter. He was accepted as a member of the Watercolour Society in Pall Mall in 1823.

It was on the advice of his brother-in-law, the architect Anthony Salvin, that Nesfield turned to landscape gardening. He began by designing formal gardens to accompany the Elizabethan- and Jacobean-style houses which Salvin was working on at the time, but soon became so well established that he no longer needed Salvin's assistance. By October 1854, when he came to Witley for three days to confer on preliminary matters with Lord Ward, he was advising some of the wealthiest and most influential landowners in the country. Sometimes these associations were maintained for decades rather than years, not only because of Nesfield's ability to design intricate and elegant parterres but because his engineering and artistic background enabled him to advise on all aspects of the landscape.

## Nesfield's design for Witley Court

Lord Ward had both the wealth and the inclination to turn Witley into one of the finest country estates in Europe. In the process all traces of George Repton's earlier work were swept away. The gardens were designed to be a perfect foil to the Italianate mansion, encompassing the south and east fronts of the house. The grandest design was to the south, where a flight of steps with a curved balustrade led down from Nash's portico. A stone balustrade with steps enclosed the formal garden, separating it from the informal deer park beyond. A central avenue led to the Perseus and Andromeda fountain and then to elaborate gates which were erected

*Nesfield's design for the south parterre is fully realised in this photograph of about 1870*

NESFIELD ARCHIVES

*Watercolour by Nesfield of the Perseus and Andromeda fountain*

to commemorate Queen Victoria's Silver Jubilee; these had been exhibited at the Paris Exhibition of 1862 and were known locally as 'The Golden Gates', having originally been gilded. The stone terminals featured carved lions' heads, presumably to echo the two stone lions that guarded the portico steps, and supported garland decorations surmounted by two stone vases decorated with flowers and swags. Two stone pavilions completed the design.

The strictly formal design of a parterre is designed to be looked down on from the most important rooms of a house; here it

NATIONAL MONUMENTS RECORD

*The Golden Gates (now in Arizona) which once terminated the south parterre*

could also be admired from the portico steps and raised ground within the balustrades. In keeping with the Italianate feel of the gardens, the parterres and shrub borders were enclosed with clipped evergreens – Portugal laurels, cypresses and yew – cut into pyramids and cones. The shrub beds and the two parterres were outlined by stone kerbs, a material favoured by Nesfield over the usual box if his client was rich enough, as it saved on time and manpower. He was particularly anxious about the use of blue gravel since at Stoke Edith in Herefordshire, a previous commission, it had been found to be poisonous to plants. This time, however, Nesfield was able to obtain a reliable supply from a quarry in Yorkshire.

## The fountains

Nesfield's greatest contribution to Witley Court was the fountains, in particular the Perseus and Andromeda fountain. His use of mythological figures was inspired by the fountains and statues of late fifteenth-century Italy, which often took Greek and Roman legends as their subjects. These in turn derived from ancient Roman sites that were being excavated at the time,

*The Perseus and Andromeda fountain in operation, c. 1870*

such as the villa of the Emperor Hadrian at Tivoli. Figures relating to the sea were, not surprisingly, thought to be highly appropriate for fountains. The myth behind the Perseus and Andromeda fountain is well known: Perseus, having

*The statuary on the fountain still inspires awe today*

obtained the head of Medusa with the help of his winged sandals and his helmet of invisibility, flies to the rescue of Andromeda, who has been tied to a rock by Poseidon, angry at the suggestion that she is more beautiful than the sea nymphs. A sea monster threatens to devour Andromeda, but before it can do so Perseus carries her off – in this case on the back of the winged horse Pegasus.

The fountain is reputed to be the largest in Europe and during the heyday of the Dudleys it played twice a week. It was carved in Portland stone by James Forsyth, while two sea nymphs, featuring as outriders, were carved by another sculptor favoured by Nesfield, T Raymond Smith. The engineers, Easton & Co, had also worked with Nesfield on previous commissions, including Holkham Hall in Norfolk and Castle Howard in Yorkshire. Four thousand gallons (18,000 litres) of water were pumped from the nearby Hundred Pool to a reservoir over half a mile (about 1km) away and 100ft (30m) above the level of the house. It was driven by a 40-horse-power steam engine, a beam pumping engine coupled to two Cornish boilers. This water supplied the fountain and the main jet, which issued from the sea monster's open mouth; the latter is reputed to have reached a height of 120ft (36m). There were numerous subsidiary jets and sprays. The dolphins had reeds fitted inside their open mouths which could be adjusted to make varying pitches of sound as the water jets issued from them (another Italian notion). Beneath the fountain were three chambers, reached by a passageway which started just outside the balustraded grounds.

## The east garden

To the east of the house was a smaller garden containing a more conventional parterre. This featured all the elements of a 'Parterre de Broderie', a type of parterre designed to look like a piece of embroidery. The style was French in origin and very popular during the seventeenth century. It featured flowing plant-like designs of scrolls, volutes (spirals) and rays, the shapes being laid out with box and filled in with coloured gravels and flowers. Like the garden on the south side of the house, it could be looked down on, this time from the ballroom. The east garden also contained clipped evergreens, ornamental shrubs and tazzas (ornamental bowls) filled with flowers. To the right of the composition was a long guilloche (a ribbon of flowers).

To add height to the design Nesfield

NESFIELD ARCHIVES

*Drawing by Nesfield showing a 'proposed enlargement of Tritons' tails' on the Flora fountain*

incorporated a smaller fountain at the terminus of the parterre. Known as the Flora fountain, this featured a statue of Flora, the goddess of Spring, standing on a pedestal with a jet of water issuing from a cornucopia (horn) which she holds on high. She is surrounded by four Tritons blowing jets from conches. According to legend, Triton was the son of Poseidon and Amphithia; here they are depicted as fishes with human heads and torsos.

PARDOE COLLECTION

*The east garden with the guilloche in the foreground*

There are smaller jets around the 164ft (50m) circumference of the basin. During the house's abandonment the fountain was vandalised, and only a fragmentary portion of Flora still remains, though a reproduction of the original statue is now in preparation.

## Nesfield as artist

Nesfield strived to transfer the art of painting into his garden designs, using what he described as 'Nature's Materials' – not only trees, shrubs and flowers, but also rocks and minerals – to add colour to his parterres during the winter months. The parterres he designed throughout his career showed off his skills as a draughtsman and surveyor: they were intricate and elegant, with a subtle blending of colours, very different from the garish bedding-out beloved of parks departments later in the Victorian age. He took his inspiration from the grand French creations of the late sixteenth and early seventeenth centuries. Sadly, few of Nesfield's grand designs have survived, having been swept away when fashions changed and money and labour were no longer available to maintain them. With the restoration of the gardens at Witley Court it is hoped that one of Nesfield's most sumptuous creations will once again flourish for all to admire.

Nesfield has in the past been underrated, especially for the wider landscapes he developed. This is where his true skills as an artist of the 'picturesque' school are evident. While he believed that the area in the immediate environs of the house should be as formal and symmetrical as possible, its boundary clearly marked by balustrades and gates, he treated the distant landscape as he would a painting. He did not favour the belts and clumps of trees beloved of Lancelot Brown, nor did he think, with Humphry Repton, that the approach to a house should be contrived so that one came upon it unexpectedly. On the contrary, he believed that drives and avenues should be straight and should terminate in a focal point – at Witley the great fountains. The landscape should be opened up to reveal distant prospects of hills: Nesfield did not hesitate to adopt what he termed 'the judicial use of the axe' if he thought it necessary. At Crewe Hall in Cheshire he had 1000 trees cut down so that the distant Staffordshire hills could be seen from the house. But he also planted many thousands of trees to help create his idea of an 'artistical perspective'.

## The gardens in Witley's heyday

When the second Earl of Dudley took up residence in 1888 the curtain was raised

*Clipped evergreens added to the Italianate feel of the gardens – a perfect foil to the house*

*The site of the south parterre today. Plans are under way for the reinstatement of key elements of Nesfield's design*

on what was to prove a *belle époque* for Witley Court. The theatrical backdrop Nesfield had provided earlier in the century was in keeping with the lifestyle that was lived here over the next few glittering decades. In particular, the east garden, with its Flora fountain, its formal parterre, flowers, tazzas and shrubs, must have provided a suitably glamorous background to the scenes of festivity in the ballroom. It is not difficult to imagine the earl and countess's guests strolling about this lovely garden on a warm summer's evening, while the fountains played, sending up a veil of spray.

By the 1890s, however, the exuberant bedding-out beloved of the later Victorians had, to some extent, replaced Nesfield's more sophisticated and elegant designs. We are told that one large bed contained 5000 geraniums set off by yellow calceolarias and blue lobelia. Also during this era, on the west side of the house, Lady Rachel laid out a small topiary garden known as 'My Lady's Garden' (see page 15).

In 1964 the two fountains had a building preservation order placed on them. Unfortunately, the Town and Country Planning Act of 1968 rescinded the order, but in 1970 the fountains were designated Ancient Monuments and in 1972 the whole estate was put in the care of the Department of the Environment, thus ensuring that they could not be demolished. Before this, however, two film stars – Bing Crosby and Stewart Granger – showed an interest in buying the fountains and even agreed a figure of £70,000, proposing to set them up at their racecourse in Chicago. Billy Butlin, the owner of Butlin's Holiday Camps, also coveted them for his home at Ascot, and at one stage they were offered to the City of Worcester. Fortunately these proposals came to nothing – although the two sea nymphs disappeared, presumably at this time. In 1968 it was estimated that to replace the Perseus and Andromeda fountain alone would cost £100,000.

Ultimately what remained of the gardens was left to slumber on in relative peace. Today, the Court and its gardens act as a magnet for many thousands of visitors each year, fascinated by the air of mystery that surrounds them.

# A Tour of Witley Court

*The north front*

## Forecourt

A visit to Witley Court begins in the forecourt outside the front entrance to the house. Most of the ground floor can be toured with the exception of the west wing, to your right, which has still to be consolidated.

Before you stands the main entrance to the Court. In the nineteenth century the forecourt was entirely gravelled to provide a turning circle for carriages. (This feature is soon to be reinstated.) Before the break-up of the estate the house enjoyed an open view towards the 'Front Pool' on the far side of the drive, behind you.

As you walk towards the main entrance notice how the red brick of the original Jacobean house can be seen where the Victorian Bath stone 'skin' (designed by the architect William Daukes for the first Earl of Dudley in the mid-nineteenth century) has fallen away.

Although it now blends in with the overall design of the exterior, the entrance portico was actually added to the house earlier in the nineteenth century for the Foley family by John Nash in about 1806. The detailing of the Ionic capitals can be seen to be purer and more refined than the work of some fifty years later: compare it with the elaborate ornament surrounding the entrance door and windows.

## Entrance Hall

The Entrance Hall of the Victorian house stretched across the full width of the building. It extended from the grand stairs, which were behind the bricked-up opening in the end wall to your right, to a point level with the east tower, to your left. In the Jacobean house part of this area would have been occupied by the Great Hall, probably rising through two storeys –

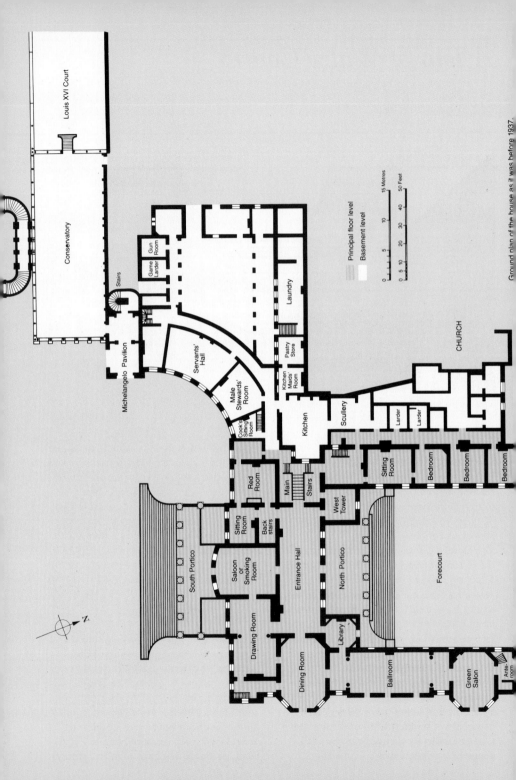

Louis XVI Court

Conservatory

Michelangelo Pavilion

Stairs

Game Larder

Gun Room

Servants' Hall

Male Stewards' Room

Cook's Sitting Room

Laundry

Pastry Store

Kitchen Maids' Room

Kitchen

Scullery

Larder

Larder

CHURCH

Red Room

Sitting Room

Back stairs

Main Stairs

West Tower

Sitting Room

Bedroom

Bedroom

Bedroom

Saloon or Smoking Room

South Portico

Entrance Hall

North Portico

Forecourt

Drawing Room

Library

Ballroom

Green Salon

Ante room

Dining Room

Principal floor level

Basement level

0    5    10                        15 Metres

0  5  10   20   30   40   50 Feet

N

Ground plan of the house as it was before 1937.

*The Entrance Hall looking west in 1882. The front door was on the right with the way through to the Saloon opposite*

an arrangement which had survived from medieval houses in general, and possibly in this case from the medieval house on the site of Witley Court itself. Beneath the concrete floor laid down in the 1970s are the remains of the medieval undercroft (see page 18). Until about 1730 this central block of the house was only one room thick (the original Witley can be imagined as being roughly 'H'-shaped in plan, with the two lower strokes extended into the long wings flanking the entrance forecourt. You are now standing in the central stroke of the 'H'). Evidence of the Jacobean hall is apparent in the blocked mullion-and-transom window to the left of the door opposite the entrance.

Sections of mid-nineteenth-century wall decoration made to look like panelling (known as 'Carton Pierre' decoration – see page 29) survive to the right of the door. Through the door and across what was the Saloon beyond is a view of the immense Perseus and Andromeda fountain sculpted by James Forsyth in 1857–60.

The opening at the right-hand end of the hall, now bricked up, led into the staircase hall. There was a central flight of stairs up to a landing, and two return flights to reach a balcony at first-floor level, off which opened bedrooms and also the

Picture Gallery which occupied almost the entire first floor of the west wing. This had replaced the Jacobean Long Gallery. The supports for the Entrance Hall balcony can be seen on the inside of the portico wall.

Behind the stairs, but at basement level, was the huge Victorian kitchen.

## West Tower

Behind you and to your right, a well-preserved early seventeenth-century doorcase leads into the West Tower. In the seventeenth and eighteenth centuries this and the corresponding east tower held staircases. Vestiges of the stairs survive between the second and third floors. More of the 'Carton Pierre' decoration can be seen here and also laths to support plaster on the walls. The reinforced concrete ring-frames were inserted during the 1970s to support the structure.

Return to the entrance hall and enter the doorway opposite to reach the small room which was the site of the servants' stairs. In the left-hand wall can be seen an

*Samuel Daukes's mid-nineteenth-century Bath stone cladding over the original Jacobean brickwork on the inner side of the east tower*

inspection hatch for the hot-air central heating system. The doorway ahead leads to the Red Sitting Room.

## Red Sitting Room

This room and the Red Room beyond would have been used as private sitting rooms. Surrounding the nineteenth-century doorway in the right-hand wall is the outline of the outer side of a seventeenth-century window. Further evidence that this was once an exterior wall exists in the finely laid stone 'quoins' in the adjacent corner abutting the south front.

## Red Room

The doorway to your right connects with the Red Room. This area was originally a short wing at the south-west corner of the Jacobean house (on the left in the picture on page 18). By turning and craning your neck upwards towards the upper section of the wall through which you have entered, you can begin to appreciate the complex changes in the roof structure over nearly

three centuries. Ghostly remains of a pattern can be seen on the opposite wall. The route to the Red Sitting Room and the Red Room was curious in that it passed through the service stairs.

## East Tower

Return to the Entrance Hall and continue to the far end of the room (marked by an information panel). An opening on the left leads into the East Tower. This too is internally braced with reinforced concrete. In the nineteenth century the original stairs were removed to create a route into the Ballroom which bypassed the Dining Room – the arch into the Ballroom (now blocked) can be seen. This small area is labelled as the Library on late Victorian plans of the house.

## Dining Room

This octagonal room occupied the far end of the building, extending into the bay window. The windows give a view of the east parterre garden with the Flora fountain

*The Dining Room in 1920. Some of the decoration still clings to the walls after sixty years' exposure to the weather*

at its centre. (The missing figure of Flora is being recarved and there are plans for the restoration of the ornamental garden.) Note that the fountain is not on the axis of the central opening of the bay, as one might expect. More of the 'Carton Pierre' moulded decoration survives on the wall.

## Ballroom

A large opening in the north wall of the Dining Room leads into the Ballroom. The Dudleys' magnificent Louis XIV-style ballroom replaced an equally splendid library dating from the Foleys' ownership of the house. The ballroom extended almost the full length of the east wing. The ceiling was higher than those of the other rooms on the ground floor to accommodate the huge chandeliers. The upper floor was supported on iron beams, some of which are still in place. The fire of 1937 created the greatest damage in this area, as the charred window timbers bear witness. In old photographs windows are shown on the exterior of the ballroom facing the forecourt, but in fact they were 'blind', and out of synchronisation with the internal panelling.

## Green Salon

Situated beyond the Ballroom, this is another octagonal room mirroring the Dining Room. It was perhaps used by guests who preferred less energetic pursuits than the dancing in the Ballroom. An 'ante-room' at the far end of the wing contained a staircase descending to a sunken bath in the basement, possibly dating from the Foley era.

## Drawing Room

Return through the Ballroom and cross the end of the Entrance Hall to reach the Drawing Room. The photograph on page 42, taken from the right-hand end, shows its appearance in 1920. In the nineteenth century a wall of the original south-east wing was removed to create a spacious but rather low room – dictated by the ceiling height of the Jacobean and Georgian periods. Another reminder of

PARDOE COLLECTION

*The magnificent Ballroom, scene of lavish dances and entertainments. Virtually nothing of this splendour survived the fire*

*The Drawing Room*

the early house is the back of the early seventeenth-century chimneystack on the inner wall; this can also be seen to the right of the central door in the picture on page 18. The remains of two mid-nineteenth-century firegrates are at first-floor level.

*A mid-nineteenth-century firegrate surviving at first-floor level. The surrounding marble mantelpiece has been removed*

## Saloon

Through the opening at the right-hand end of the Drawing Room, in the centre of the south front, is the Saloon. Yet more 'Carton Pierre' decoration survives here. The Saloon and adjacent rooms must have been well shaded and even a little dark behind the deep south portico.

The Saloon came to be used mainly as a 'passage room' leading to the garden – an arrangement typical of Victorian country house planning. Walk through to the south portico and look back at the bow front of the Saloon. The upper part was left untouched by the Victorian stone casing of the house because it was screened by the portico. The elaborate decoration above the central doorway has recently been recarved as a result of a private donation from Miss Barbara Mapstone of Cheltenham.

## South portico

This is a twin of the portico on the north front and was also designed by John Nash. The floor was originally paved with black-and-white marble squares. It provides a fine elevated platform from which to view the south parterre garden, dominated by the

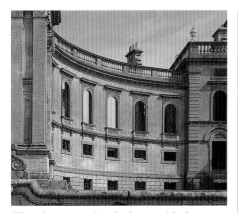

*The wing connecting the house with the conservatory. It contained the nursery and servants' accommodation*

Perseus and Andromeda fountain. The basin from which this gigantic sculpture rises has recently been reflooded and the fountain will soon be in operation. The balusters flanking the stone steps to the garden have also been replaced. Stone lions in poses of terrifying anger once rested on the plinths at the foot of the terrace.

The curving wing to the right of the portico is entirely mid-nineteenth-century and dates from Samuel Daukes's alterations. Only the outer wall survives but before the fire it housed the servants' hall at the lower level, with the nursery, schoolroom and governess's accommodation above.

## Michelangelo Pavilion

Cross to the building at the end of the curving wing, which formed the entrance to the conservatory. Loosely based on the Capitoline Museum in Rome (c.1539) by Michelangelo Buonarroti, this is one of the best preserved parts of the Court. It has a fine tesselated floor and a niche for a statue at the far end.

## Conservatory

Sometimes referred to as the Orangery, the conservatory was as big as a Victorian

*The skeleton of Daukes's vast conservatory. It was once filled with tropical plants*

railway station and rather resembled one, albeit containing abundant foliage (see photograph on page 14). Remains of the thick plate glass can still be seen inserted directly into the columns without conventional window frames. The stone baskets of flowers on the rear wall were carved by James Forsyth and reveal a French influence. Forsyth was also responsible for the most important stone masonry on the house, such as the capitals (at the tops of the columns) and tympana (over the doors), together with the two great fountains. The camellia growing up the wall is an original plant dating from before the fire, and is therefore at least sixty years old. The stone block near the centre once supported an ornamental urn.

## Louis XVI Court

The French influence is carried through into this appropriately named area, where

*One of two domed pavilions in the south parterre garden*

fruit trees might have been trained up the sheltered walls. The niche in the far wall once contained a statue which is now at Harlaxton Manor, Lincolnshire.

## The south parterre garden
*(see also pages 31–4)*

On either side of the south garden are domed pavilions in what might be described as a Hindu style, designed by Samuel Daukes. On the hill at the centre of the low encircling wall stood magnificent gates of gilded wrought iron; these are now in Arizona.

Continue on around the outside of the house, through the east parterre garden where you can see the Flora fountain, and return to the north front.

## The Church
*The church is not in the care of English Heritage but is the responsibility of the Parochial Church Council. It is maintained by the local community and the entrance charge to Witley Court does not contribute to its upkeep.*

The remarkable church of St Michael and All Angels, Great Witley is one of the high points of any visit to Witley Court. It stands prominently on high ground to the west of the ruins of the house and appears at first to be the surviving private chapel of the great house. In fact, it was and still is the parish church.

The patron of the church was the first Lord Foley, while the man responsible for its fine baroque decoration and glass was the second Lord Foley. The original thirteenth-century parish church was replaced, since it was said to be 'by reason of its antiquity ... ruinouse and much decayed'. It is believed that the architect may have been James Gibbs. (Lord Foley had been a commissioner on Queen Anne's new churches campaign, to which Gibbs had contributed designs.)

*St Michael and All Angels: one of the finest baroque church interiors in Britain*

Alternatively the church may have been designed by Francis Smith of Warwick. Work eventually began after the death of Lord Foley.

The church is a stately, but relatively plain rectangular building. The east end projects slightly to north and south, and at the west end is a square tower, surmounted by an open cupola. The whole was encased in Bath stone by Daukes in the 1850s. As *The Buildings of England: Worcestershire* says: 'Enter and you are transported into a different climate. Here is the most Italian ecclesiastic space in the whole of England.' The richness of the building's interior derives from another great house of the eighteenth century, Canons at Edgware, the palace of the Duke of Chandos. The chapel there was designed by James Gibbs and decorated with paintings by Antonio Bellucci (1654–1726) and gilded stucco by Giovanni Bagutti (1681–1730). The twelve painted windows were by an English artist, Joshua Price (d.1722). Daniel Defoe wrote that the chapel was a 'singularity, not only in its building and the beauty of its workmanship, but in ... that the duke maintains there a full choir, and has the worship performe'd ... with the best musick (with Handel as Kappelmeister) after the manner of the chapel royal which is not done in any other nobel man's chappel in Britain.' The architect Vanbrugh wrote to the Duke of Newcastle in September 1720: 'To deal justly with his magnificence, we found nothing at all in it Ridiculous or Foppish as people have Represented.'

In 1747 Canons was demolished and Lord Foley bought at auction most of the important decorative fittings: the paintings by Bellucci – including the central ceiling panel depicting the Ascension; and painted glass, depicting the life of Christ, painted by Joshua Price after *modelli* by Sleter. The ceiling is after a design by Gibbs, which it has been suggested was based on that of Canons, but adapted for the Witley church. The decoration was carried out in a newly patented form of papier mâché stucco and incorporates rococo decoration not shown in Gibbs's drawing. There is no documentary evidence for the long-held belief that the Canons chapel ceiling was recast by the use of moulds. The pulpit, pews and panelling were removed to the church of Fawley in Buckinghamshire. The distinguished monument in the south transept to the first Baron Foley and his family was designed and carved in 1753 by J M Rysbrack (1694–1770) at a cost of £2000. The design survives in the Victoria and Albert Museum.

Most of the present fittings such as pews, pulpit and font were introduced in the mid-nineteenth century, to designs by Samuel Daukes for William Humble Ward, the first Earl of Dudley. Two brothers, William and James Forsyth, carried out most of the carving. These nineteenth-century additions fit remarkably well with the baroque decoration of the previous century. The eighteenth-century balustrade leading to the pulpit was discreetly incorporated into the nineteenth-century carved pulpit. In 1913 Venetian mosaics by Salviati & Co were introduced to the altarpiece.

The church was not damaged at all

*J M Rysbrack's 1753 monument to the first Baron Foley and his family*

by the fire at the house in 1937, but was sadly neglected after Witley Court was left uninhabited. In 1962 parishioners realised that the building would be irreparably damaged by damp and decay if immediate action were not taken. A restoration programme was begun and is continuing, thus ensuring the survival of this unique parish church.

# The Future

*The Perseus and Andromeda fountain, one of the most memorable sights of Witley Court*

After the Department of the Environment took Witley Court into guardianship in 1972 a programme of work to consolidate the structure was implemented. The results can be seen today in the reinforced concrete frames in the towers and porticos, and the concrete raft inserted at the principal floor level to facilitate public access to most of the house.

Since the building came into the custody of English Heritage in 1984, more work has been done on reinstating the south portico steps and sections of the balustrading around the roof. Recently work has been done to restore the cupola above the stableyard gatehouse and the Flora fountain in the east garden. In 1995 the basin of the great Perseus and Andromeda fountain was waterproofed

and reflooded. The spectacular fountains have not been operational for nearly sixty years, although a test demonstration of the Perseus and Andromeda fountain in 1992 drew in a huge crowd.

Support from the Heritage Lottery Fund has enabled English Heritage to begin the repair of the two great gardens, putting back the fallen balustrading and paths, and replacing much of the lost framework planting to recreate the essence of Nesfield's great garden. It is intended that the sculpture on the two fountains will be repaired and they will soon be restored to working order. The north parterre has already been recreated, the carriage sweep to the north portico restored, and part of the balustrade rebuilt to repair the setting of the house in its parkland. The bank

*A panorama from the south, photographed in 1995*

between the Front Pool has been cleared of recent planting to open up views of the lake.

It is intended to complete the repair of the house and to mitigate the effects of some of the earlier repairs, which though essential at the time are not in keeping with the importance of the building. The ruinous buildings of the stable court still remain to be repaired, though work on the stable gate is well advanced with its cupola restored. Following completion of this work, the clock mechanism, which was removed to the church tower by Daukes in the 1860s, will be reinstated on its original site. The adjacent stable buildings will be repaired to allow public access to this fascinating area. Other projects include public access to the basements of the building and to the kitchen.

English Heritage acquired land on the north of the drive with generous support from the Heritage Lottery Fund. Before the break-up of the parkland, this area comprised the late eighteenth-century wilderness, the largest of the five lakes in the park, the cascade, the boathouse, and a remarkable valley garden. Repair of this area is now largely complete, with much of

the wilderness replanted, incorporating a new access road, car park and visitor facilities in an area where modern development had destroyed the historic landscape.

The experience of visiting Witley should be enormously enhanced by these developments. The restoration of the parterre gardens and fountains is particularly exciting and will result in what may be the largest and most splendid sequence of Victorian country house formal gardens in Britain.

*The Front Pool looking west*